FOREWORD

Welcome to this first book of camp fire
stunts, compiled from letters sent in by
readers of Scouting Magazine.

It has long been a tradition in the Scout
Movement to hold camp fires, in the course
of which entertainment is put on by Cubs,
Scouts and their Leaders. This book is
offered as resource material for such
entertainment, but many of the items could
also be used as the basis for material
for scout shows, reviews etc. We feel
sure that a lot of the ideas will be new
to people outside the Movement and may
well be helpful to anybody producing some
form of light entertainment or show.

We hope that this will be the first of
several publications. If you have a
favourite sketch or camp fire hint that
you would like to offer, please send it
to David Saint, care of :-

6 Angel Hill Drive, Sutton, Surrey SM1 3BX

TECHNIQUES

The main aim of a camp fire stunt is to entertain, to make people laugh. There are many ways of doing this, and whole books have been written on the subject. There are, however, a number of useful points to bear in mind.

1. The unexpected. This has always been a very popular technique with comedians and, if carefully used, can be extremely effective. As you go through this book of stunts you will find, for example, that many of them are aimed at making the participants look foolish or, more likely, just wet! A stunt which obviously sets out to do this and then at the last moment is altered so that someone completely different suffers, will generally be funnier than simply seeing the expected victim put his feet in the expected bucket of water.

2. Timing. This is really the key to success and is something which is practiced over and over again by all entertainers. The funniest sketch can be ruined either by being drawn out for far too long with the result that the audience loses interest, or, more likely, being rushed through by a nervous entertainer who does not allow the audience time to relish the situation, or to laugh in the right places.

3. Presentation. It is always worth spending some time preparing your sketch. It is obviously much better if all the participants know their words and do not

need to rely upon pieces of paper or prompts. If the participants have really thought through the sketch and the situation it portrays an excellent result can be obtained if they are able and willing to 'ad lib' and add to the text as they go along. They should not be encouraged to do this, however, if they are unlikely to be able to hold it together.

Props are unlikely to be readily available in camp so some improvisation will be necessary. This in itself can provide plenty of humour if totally inappropriate articles are used. A seat from a portable toilet, for example, might be used as a car steering wheel, and if this is done with a completely straight face by the participant the audience will find it hard to resist a laugh. Props are not essential by any means. They can detract from the sketch, particularly if the participants are so interested in what they are wearing or carrying or using that they are not really concentrating on putting across the story line. People, particularly youngsters, have excellent imaginations and it is often only necessary for an announcer to inform them that a particular bench is now a submarine for them to be able to see it as just that.

A camp fire stunt is a splendid way to 'punctuate' a camp fire but this should not be overdone. The use of too many stunts on one occasion will weaken the effect of each of them. The trap of re-using the old favourites should also be avoided where possible. In that way they will become even more popular and successful.

The best stunts are not contained in this book at all. These are the ones which directly relate to the people present at the camp fire, their appearance, personality and the things they have been up to at camp. A topical joke is always far more successful, but beware of using this technique too much in front of an audience which is not wholly in on the joke. There have been occasions, for example, at which parents and friends have been invited to an end-of-camp camp fire and have been unable to share the uncontrolled laughter of the Cubs and Scouts at the topical sketches because they did not know what event had taken place to inspire them in the first place.

Good entertaining!

ASSORTED STUNTS

The Oasis

The scene is set by a boy standing by a bowl of water, his arms outstretched and holding ferns or other foliage in each hand. More greenery is sticking out of his clothing in an attempt to make him look like a palm tree! The narrator informs the audience that it is a baking hot day in the desert with nothing around for miles except an oasis and one solitary palm tree. One boy then crawls into the camp fire circle, dressed as raggedly as possible. He crawls towards the oasis crying :
"Water, water".
He gets near but then collapses and dies. A second and third boy repeat this process and then a fourth boy enters. He manages to reach the oasis after much effort and expresses considerable relief at having arrived. He then removes a toothbrush from his hip pocket and makes a great show of cleaning his teeth, using the water at the oasis.

Note :

This should be acted with considerable pathos and any over-acting is to be encouraged! If a number of boys are to die on the way to the oasis, it would be a good idea if considerable variety could be given to their attempts to reach the oasis and many laughs could be obtained on the way, particularly from their over-acting.

Who Wears the Trousers?

A husband and wife go to the tailor's to buy the husband a new suit. The tailor measures the man for the suit whilst asking him questions about what he wants, but each time he asks a question the wife interrupts him and answers it. For example:

Tailor : "What style do you require sir?"
Wife :   "A two piece, double breasted, with three buttons."
Tailor : "What colour material?"
Wife :   "Blue."
Tailor : "What material?"
Wife :   "Mohair."

And so on. While this is going on the husband stands there looking a bit sheepish.

Eventually the tailor tires of this and begins to measure the wife instead. The wife protests saying that the suit is for her husband, not herself. The tailor replies :

"I'm sorry madam, but I thought that you wear the trousers in your house!"

Note :

More humour could be obtained by the wife being a Cub or Scout or Leader dressed in drag.

Security Check

One boy is the sentry at the Tinpot Army Headquarters. He marches up and down smartly. A man approaches holding a note book.

Man :   "Good afternoon sir. I'm from the K.G.B. Um, er, I'm from the New York Times. I'd like some information about the Tinpot Army please."

The soldier ignores him and continues marching up and down. The man catches up with him and, jogging behind, asks his questions :

Man :   "Well, how many soldiers are there in the Tinpot Army?"
Soldier :   (After some consideration and finger counting) "About twelve."
Man :   "Um, can I borrow your pen please?"

The soldier gives him a pen and continues his marching.

Each time the man asks a question, the soldier stops marching to consider it before giving his answer.

Man :   "How many officers are there?"
Soldier :   "About twelve."
Man :   "How many tanks have you got?"
Soldier :   "About twelve."
Man :   "How many jeeps have you got?"
Soldier :   "About twelve."
Man :   "How many aeroplanes have you got?"
Soldier :   (After long consideration) "About two."

```
Man       :  "How many machine guns have you
             got?"
Soldier   : "About twelve."
Man       :  "How many ships has the navy
             got?"
Soldier   : (Without any consideration) "One."
Man       :  "How many torpedoes have they
             got?"
Soldier   : (Without any consideration) "What
             torpedoes?"
Man       :  "How many anti-aircraft guns
             have you got?"
Soldier   : "About twelve."
Man       :  "Well now.  Thank you very much,
             that was very helpful."
```

He begins to move off.

```
Soldier   : "Halt!  You thought you had got
             away with it, didn't you?  I'm
             not so easily fooled you know.
             I know what you wanted all along,
             and you're not getting away with
             it.  Give me my pen back!"
```

Fire!

A hotel guest walks into the camp fire circle and says to the waiter :

"Excuse me, could I have a glass of water?"

The waiter gives him a mug of water. The guest goes out and the waiter continues to pretend to serve meals. The guest returns and requests another glass of water which is provided, and the guest leaves again. This happens a number of times and eventually the waiter asks if the guest is particularly thirsty. The guest replies :

"No, my bedroom is on fire."

Is it Safe?

The scene is a station in the wilds of Siberia. An old station master sits dozing by the side of the track. A traveller enters the camp fire circle, wakes the station master and asks :
"Are there any trains going North today?"
The station master says :
"No, there are no trains going North today."
The traveller goes and sits down.

Another traveller enters from another part of the circle and also wakes up the station master and enquires whether any trains are going South today. The station master replies that no trains are going South today.

The second traveller joins the first, and a third traveller enters to ask whether any trains are travelling East today. The station master replies that no trains are travelling East today, and the third traveller joins the other two.

A fourth then enters from another part of the circle and asks whether any trains are travelling West today. The staiton master replies somewhat impatiently that no trains are travelling West today so all four travellers rise and say together:

"Well, in that case, it must be safe to cross the line" and they do so.

The Medicine Machine

The scene is a Red Indian encampment where the local medicine man is holding his 'surgery'. He announces that he has a magnificent new medicine machine. He calls in the first patient.

First patient : "Doctor, can you do anything about my leg?"
Medicine Man : "Yes, I think so. Let's try this new machine."
He calls out loudly :
"Poison Arrow."

Poison Arrow appears wearing a wierd mask and he and the first patient take hold of opposite ends of the machine. The medicine man operates the machine and the patient shakes his leg, and says :

"That's cleared it - my leg is better. Thank you doctor."

And he walks off. Poison Arrow turns and limps off stage. The doctor then calls in a second patient who has a jerking arm. The same process is repeated and once the machine has been operated, the patient's arm stops jerking, but Poison Arrow's arm jerks instead.

This can be repeated with any number of patients and maladies. The final patient enters, dressed as a pregnant squaw, and asks the doctor whether he can do anything to help her. When Poison Arrow is called on he enters slowly, limping, with his arm jerking, and the symptoms of various other ailments. He takes one look at the pregnant squaw and cries out :

"Oh no, not that!"

and rushes off stage.

Note :

The medicine machine can be as wierd and
wonderful as you like, maybe with sound
effects and other special effects.

QUICKIES

What's up Doc?

One boy enters the camp fire just as a previous item is closing and looks up to the sky. He remains in that position. Another boy enters and looks to see what the first boy is looking at. Another follows suit and another. Eventually the last boy asks :
"What are we looking at?"
The boy he asks doesn't know and the question is repeated down the line. When the first boy is asked the question, he replies :
"Nothing mate, I've got a stiff neck!"

Just in Case

One boy enters the camp fire circle, carrying a briefcase which he shows to the audience. The master of ceremonies asks him :
"What are you up to?"
The Scout replies :
"I'm taking my case to court!"
Later the same Scout re-enters, still carrying the case but being carried by a second boy. The master of ceremonies asks impatiently :
"What are you doing now?"
The Scout replies :
"I'm taking my case to a higher court!"
Finally the Scout re-enters without the briefcase, looking all around the ground. The master of ceremonies asks even more impatiently what he is doing, and the Scout replies :
"I lost my case!"

Don't Fall for this One

A voice from outside the camp fire circle calls out :
"Help! Help! I'm stuck in a 40' palm tree."
The master of ceremonies sounding surprised replies :
"What? You're stuck in a 40' palm tree?"
The voice replies :
"Yes! Help!"
The master of ceremonies calls back :
"But there are no 40' palm trees around here."
The voice says anxiously :
"There aren't?"
The master of ceremonies replies :
"No."
The audience then hears a falling scream and a loud thump.

Wood You Believe It?

Two boys enter carrying a large piece of wood. The master of ceremonies asks them:
"Where are you going?"
The Scouts reply :
"We are bored."
Two Scouts enter the camp fire circle carrying a large piece of wood each. The master of ceremonies asks :
"Where are you going now?"
The Scouts reply :
"Oh! We're going to a board meeting."
Two Scouts enter carrying one large plank with a small Scout lying stiffly upon it.
The master of ceremonies asks :
"What's wrong with him?"
The Scouts reply :
"He's bored stiff!"

The Other Man's Grass

The commentator explains to the audience that the scene is a country lane surrounded by fields. He should eloquently describe the peaceful nature of the area, the birds singing, the bees humming, the sun shining. It is a glorious day. He then stands back and two drunks enter, singing, staggering about, and leaning on each other. They slump down on the floor in a drunken stupor. The commentator steps forward and continues to describe the scene and announces that at this moment a horse is pulling a cart full of hay slowly along the lane. The drunks sit up and watch it go by and one drunk says to the other :
"That's what I'm going to do when I get rich."
The second drunk asks :
"What's that?"
The first drunk replies :
"Send my grass away to be cut!"

It's no Joke

Two boys sit opposite each other on the floor six feet apart with a cup of water mid way between them. They sit and look at each other for about thirty seconds, without moving, and without smiling. Eventually one boy slowly picks up the cup and slings the water in the other boy's face. He sits down again. After about thirty seconds the second boy asks :

"Was that some kind of joke?"

After another thirty seconds the first boy replies :

"No."

After another thirty seconds the second boy replies :

"That's O.K. then. I don't like that kind of joke!"

VICTIMS

It would seem that a significant proportion of camp fire stunts are aimed at making either the unsuspecting participants or audience look foolish or, better still, drenched! This section therefore contains no less than eight stunts along these lines but we would ask that they are used with consideration! The victims and the occasion should be chosen with care as a practical joke becomes a lot less funny if the victim is unlikely to take it in good part and becomes very upset or agitated. It is particularly hard for a new and young member of the Section to be made fun of in front of his colleagues, and in a strange setting away from home.

The Greatest Shop in the World

The shopkeeper walks into the centre of the camp fire circle. He says :
"Let me introduce myself. I am (insert name) the owner of the greatest shop in the world. My shop has everything you could possibly want in stock, and in the unlikely event that I haven't got what you want, my warehouse will send it over immediately."
At this point a customer enters the shop.
Shopkeeper : "Can I help you sir?"
Customer : "Yes, I would like a set of six cups and saucers."
Shopkeeper : "Of course sir, one moment."

The shopkeeper turns away and pretends to look on some shelves.
Shopkeeper : "Oh dear. I'm sorry sir, I appear to have sold them all, but I can have some sent over immediately. If you would like to call back shortly?"
Customer : "O.K. Thank you."
Shopkeeper : "Whilst I'm waiting for the cups and saucers to arrive let me show you (the audience) some of the items in my shop. Can I have two volunteers?"
Two volunteers are then selected.
Shopkeeper : "One of the many things I have in my shop are light bulbs and these two are going to show you how they work."
The shopkeeper describes to the two volunteers what they must do :
"You must squat down then leap up with your arms and legs spread out and shout "ping"."
The two volunteers start to carry out these actions and are asked to continue them throughout the sketch. The customer returns.

"Have those cups and saucers arrived yet?"
Shopkeeper : "Oh dear, they're not in yet.
Could you try again in about an hour's
time?"
Customer : "Yes, alright, but please
be sure they're here by then."
Shopkeeper : "Yes sir, thank you. Now I'll
show you all something else."
He recruits two more volunteers.
Shopkeeper : "I also sell washing machines.
You two must pretend to use a scrubbing
board and bend down whilst you're doing
it because it's hard work. You have to
say "rub a dub dub"."
The boys playing the part of the light
bulbs are then joined by the boys playing
the washing machines and the four continue
the actions together. The customer returns.
"Are those cups and saucers in yet?"
Shopkeeper : "Uh, no. I'm really sorry
about this but they're having to make up
a new set for you. I'll definitely have
them in by the morning."
Customer : "Alright, but this is your
last chance." He leaves.
The shopkeeper obtains two more volunteers
and informs the audience that he also sells
teapots. These two volunteers are asked
to place their left hand on their hip as
the teapot handle, and arch their right
hand and arm like a spout and rock forward
saying "I'm a teapot." These two volunteers
join the other four making a total of six
carrying out a variety of extraordinary
actions. The customer returns.
"Where are my cups and saucers?"
Shopkeeper : "I'm very sorry sir but it
has been quite impossible for us to obtain
any but I can offer you these six mugs."
He points to the volunteers.

My Kingdom for a Horse

A blanket is laid down and one boy kneels on it praying to Allah. He bows down and touches his head on the floor and says "Oh Allah, give me a camel."
After repeating this a few times he looks under the blanket and shakes his head sadly. He then asks for a volunteer to help him pray. The two kneel down together, bow down touch their heads on the blanket and say :
"Oh Allah, give us a camel."
After a few more repetitions they look under the blanket and shake their heads sadly and the first boy asks for another volunteer. This can be repeated until there are perhaps five or six people, all praying for a camel. Eventually the first person stands up and looks at the volunteers all kneeling on the blanket and bowing and chanting together. He shakes his head and says :
"Well, Allah hasn't given us a camel but he has given us a lot of silly asses."

The Skiing Lesson

This stunt is suitable for a Six or Patrol of perhaps six boys to prepare in advance. The Sixer or Patrol Leader offers the services of his boys as skiing instructors. Six volunteers from the audience are recruited and each one receives personal instruction from one of the Six or Patrol. They are taught how to step sideways, how to bend the knee and how to sway down the slopes. Then the Leader informs them that they have to learn how to ski in the dark and they are asked to turn and face the audience whilst the "instructors" put their hands over the learners' eyes so that it seems to be night time. The learners then carry out the side stepping and knee bending and swaying which they have learned. When the lesson is over and the instructors remove their hands the skiers may not be aware that anything has changed. It has, however, as each instructor had cocoa powder on his hands and each skier now has two black eyes!

The Ugliest Person in the World

The announcer brings into the camp fire circle a person covered with a blanket. He announces that under this blanket is the ugliest person in the world. He invites members of the audience to come and take a look at this person if they dare and the first few people to volunteer should be those boys "in the know". Each of these comes up in turn, takes a quick look under the blanket, screams and faints. There is plenty of scope for over-acting here! After four or five boys have been suitably horrified by the sight behind the blanket an unsuspecting person is invited to look. This might be a Leader, a particularly troublesome boy, or perhaps the visiting Commissioner! When the blanket is lifted and the volunteer and the ugliest person in the world come face to face it is the turn of the ugliest person in the world to scream and collapse in a heap on the ground.

The Submarine

The announcer informs the audience that he wishes to tell the story of a submarine mission. A volunteer is required to set the scene. The volunteer is asked to lie down in the middle of the camp fire circle and an old coat is placed over him. He is asked to raise one arm up through a sleeve of the coat as the periscope. The announcer tells a story about the submarine mission involving leaving port, submerging, spotting an enemy ship, firing a torpedo, coming to the surface to see what damage has been caused and then retreating beneath the surface as enemy aircraft approach.

In the course of this story there is much raising and lowering of the periscope and the volunteer raises and lowers his arm accordingly. Unfortunately on the last occasion when the enemy aircraft appear the announcer is in too much of a hurry to get the submarine below the surface and forgets to have the periscope lowered. As a result water gushes into the submarine down the raised sleeve of the coat onto the volunteer. The water is thoughtfully provided by an assistant with a cup of water.

Easy Money?

The announcer produces a bucket of water and a fifty pence piece. He invites a volunteer from the audience to attempt to retrieve the fifty pence piece from the bucket of water whilst blindfolded. This is a particularly unkind stunt and the volunteer should be carefully selected for his sense of humour! The volunteer is shown the fifty pence piece dropped into the bucket of water and is blindfolded. The bucket of water is then swiftly removed and replaced with a bucket containing the day's slops of porridge, spaghetti, rice pudding etc. If all the camp food has been devoured then a special mix can be prepared comprising mud and water. The volunteer is told that he has 15 seconds to find the fifty pence piece and in his eagerness he plunges his hand into something other than what he expected.

Oral Hygiene

Five boys line up and the first boy announces :
"This is the story of how to clean your teeth."
Second boy : "I squeeze the toothpaste onto my brush."
Third boy : "I brush my teeth from side to side."
Fourth boy : "I brush my teeth up and down."
Fifth boy : "I rinse my mouth out."
The sixth boy turns to the audience and expels water from his mouth in a suitable manner.

Note : Each boy carries out the appropriate actions.

The sketch should not last too long otherwise the fifth boy may swallow the water!

The Australian Spitting Contest

The announcer informs the audience that in the outback there is little entertainment and so the Australian cowboys have to devise their own ways of passing the time. One of these is a spitting contest in which each participant tries to spit further than any other. The spit is caught in a cup by a judge. Four boys then line up and a judge stands a little way from them holding a tin mug. The first boy pretends to spit, the judge pretends to catch the spit in the mug and flicks the bottom of it with his thumb to make it sound as if he caught it. The second boy then does the same and the judge again catches it. The third and fourth boys also make their contribution, each time the judge moving backwards or forwards accordingly. Throughout the contest the excitement mounts and at the end the judge announces the winner with great pleasure. In his excitement he throws his arms in the air and the mug (which was already half filled with water) is emptied firmly in the direction of the audience.

ACTIONS SPEAK LOUDER THAN WORDS

Many boys will be reluctant to learn a lot of words for their sketches but many sketches can take place with few or no words at all. Some action sketches can require more skill to put across than those which do rely on words and punchlines but they can be very effective indeed.

The Old Ford Car

Five Scouts are located under a ground sheet, four at the corners as the wheels of the car and one in the centre as the driving seat and engine. This boy holds a billy can with pebbles in it. All the boys are on their knees. A sixth boy enters. He is the driver. He goes to the front of the car and cranks the engine. It starts into life as the boy in the centre starts to shake the billy can and all five boys vibrate as if they were a vehicle starting up. The driver climbs into the seat but as soon as he settles down a front wheel deflates as the boy playing that part lies flat on the ground. The driver gets out and pumps up the tyre and the boy returns to his previous position. It is then necessary to re-start the engine and eventually the driver gets back into the seat, only for another tyre to go down. The process is repeated and eventually the driver has to pump up all the tyres. Once he has done this he re-starts the engine but instead of vibrating into life there is a loud bang and all the wheels fall off. An inventive team could no doubt think of other parts of the car to be represented and other parts to go wrong.

The Operation

This sketch could easily have appeared in the "Bad Taste" section!

A large sheet is set up between the audience and the actors with a bright light behind the actors to throw their shadows onto the sheet. A table is set up behind the sheet and one actor lies on it. An operation is carried out upon this person by a doctor and nurses using standard camp equipment such as bow saws, axes, mallets etc. A number of unusual items are produced from the patient's inside, including strings of sausages etc. From time to time the patient will try to get up but he should be restrained by the doctors and nurses and occasionally treated by the 'anaesthetist' with a mallet! With practice, a very convincing show can be put together so that to the audience watching the shadows it really does look as if the patient is being cut open with a bow saw and that the items are actually being produced from his stomach.

The Left Hand Does Not Know
What the Right Hand is Doing

This stunt requires a little bit of setting up. Four people are needed and for convenience we will refer to them as A, B, C and D. 'A' lies down on his back on the ground. 'B' kneels across him facing his legs and feet. 'B's arms are the arms of the new person. 'C' is a taller person than 'B' and also kneels across 'A' behind 'B'. 'C' is the face of the new person. 'D' is there to help generally. 'A', 'B' and 'C' are then covered with a blanket so that it looks as though there is one large person sitting up in bed. Only one set of arms, legs and feet and a face are showing. The fourth player, 'D', comes on stage and shakes the resting body - Mr. Brown.
"Good morning Mr. Brown."
Mr. Brown yawns and stretches his arms. 'D' then says :
"Here's the flanel to have a wash."
And he hands the wet flanel and the towel to the arms on either side of Mr. Brown.
Then 'D' hands him the toothbrush and toothpaste and he attempts to brush his teeth. This continues with combing his hair, eating his breakfast etc. It does not take much imagination to work out the problems faced by the person acting as

Mr. Brown's arms when it comes to trying
to place a spoonful of cereal into,
effectively, somebody else's mouth! In
the meantime Mr. Brown's legs can be moving
about as if they have have a life of their
own as well.

The Mortgage on the Cow

This extremely popular sketch fits uneasily into this or almost any other section of such a collection. Although there are many words to it they are simple and repetitive and easily learnt, and the sketch goes down extremely well even with those who have seen it and heard it many times before. There is plenty of scope for individualism in its presentation. The scene is a widow's cottage. She is very poor and has two sons and a daughter to bring up. Her only remaining possession is a cow and even that is mortgaged. All the words of the stunt are spoken to a strict rhythm and when a number of actors are present they all speak all the words in the same rhythm. At the same time they all bend their knees and rise again, also in rhythm with the words. The humour of the sketch arises as they gradually get out of synchronisation with each other, until by the end they are all chanting the same words to the same rhythm but bobbing up and down at different times.

The widow is on stage on her own. Her eldest son enters. He stands beside her with his hands behind his back and says:
"What's the matter Ma? What's the matter Ma?"
His mother replies :
"We aint got the money for the mortgage on the cow. We aint got the money for the mortgage on the cow. Sob, sob, sob."
The daughter enters.
"What's the matter Ma? What's the matter Ma?"
The mother and son reply together :

"We aint got the money for the mortgage on the cow. We aint got the money for the mortgage on the cow. Sob, sob, sob."
The youngest son enters.
"What's the matter Ma? What's the matter Ma?"
The mother, son and daughter all reply:
"We aint got the money for the mortgage on the cow. We aint got the money for the mortgage on the cow. Sob, sob, sob."
The debt collector enters.
"I've come to get the money for the mortgage on the cow. I've come to get the money for the mortgage on the cow."
All the family reply :
"We aint got the money for the mortgage on the cow. We aint got the money for the mortgage on the cow. Sob, sob, sob."
The debt collector replies :
"But I've got to have the money for the mortgage on the cow. But I've got to have the money for the mortgage on the cow."
The family produce guns from their pockets and shoot the debt collector. Bang, bang, bang.
The debt collector exclaims :
"Agh! Agh! Agh!"
The family chant together :
"We don't need the money for the mortgage on the cow. We don't need the money for the mortgage on the cow. Hooray, hooray, hooray."

ECHOS

The Unexpected Guest

The scene is a hotel in a mountain resort.
The first guest arrives :
"I understand you have the finest hotel
around."
The manager replies :
"Absolutely."
The second guest says :
"With good food?"
The manager :
"Absolutely."
The third guest :
"And excellent drink?"
The manager :
"Absolutely."
And so on until all the available cast
are used up. The first guest :
"But what about entertainment?"
The Manager :
"We have the most extraordinary echo in
the world."
First guest :
"Let me try. Hey there!"
Echo :
"Hey there."
The second guest :
"I'll have a go. Hallo!"
Echo :
"Hallo."
The third guest :
"How about a drink?"
Echo :
"I'll be right down."

There's been an Accident

Four boys secretly leave the camp fire
and station themselves approximately 25
yards away in each of the four corners
surrounding the camp fire. Another boy
lies down somewhere within the camp fire
circle.

A fifth boy walks into the camp fire circle
and sees the casualty lying on the ground.
He rushes over to see what's wrong, and
calls out :
"There's been an accident."
This echo is taken up by the boys hidden
around the camp fire circle, one at a time.
The boy at the scene of the accident looks
round anxiously for help and shouts out
into the darkness :
"Quick, get an ambulance."
This echo is also repeated by the four
hidden boys in turn. The boy at the scene
of the accident then shouts :
"Hurry, he's going."
First echo :
"He's going."
Second echo :
"He's going."
Third echo :
"He's going."
Fourth echo :
"He's gone."

WHAT'S IN A NAME?

Where did you get that Hat?

The first player enters the circle wearing a smart hat. A "stooge" seated in the audience calls out :
"That's a nice hat. Where did you get it?"
The person wearing the hat replies :
"I got it from John Collier."
Another boy enters wearing a coat. The stooge calls out :
"That's a nice coat. Where did you get it?"
The boy replies :
"I got it from John Collier."
This continues with various other items of clothing, until the last boy enters wearing only his swimming trunks. The stooge calls out :
"What are you playing at? Who are you?"
The boy calls back :
"I'm John Collier."

Peanuts

The scene is a court and the king is hearing various cases.
King :   "Bring in the next prisoner and state his name and charge."
The guard enters with the prisoner.
Guard :   "The prisoner's name is Jacob and his crime is throwing peanuts over the cliff."
King :   "What? Throwing peanuts over

the cliff.   Throw this man to the man-
eating ants."
The guard and prisoner exit, the prisoner
shouting in fright at hs fate.
King :   "Next."
Second guard:"This man is Jack and his
crime is also throwing peanuts over the
cliff."
King :   "This is terrible.   Throw
him to the lead-booted caterpillars."
The second guard exits with a similarly
frightened prisoner and noises of the man
being thrown into the pit are made.
King :   "This is all too much for
one day, but bring in the next one."
A man staggers in. He is crying and wailing
and all his clothes are torn.   The king
says :
"How dare you appear in front of me like
this. What's your name?"
The Man : "Please sir, my name is Peanuts."
He falls to the ground.

A Spade's a Spade

Two labourers are reading a church notice board which announces that two grave diggers are required. One labourer goes to the vicar for his interview and the vicar says:

"You can have the job if you can answer this question. Who were the first man and woman on earth?"

The labourer replies :

"That's easy. Adam and Eve."

He goes out and tells the other labourer who says :

"I don't think I'll remember that. I'll write the answer on my spade."

The second labourer goes in, is asked the same question, looks at his spade and replies :

"Spear and Jackson."

GAMES, SONGS AND HINTS

Alphabetical Stories

The camp fire leader gives each person round the fire a letter in alphabetical order. The camp fire leader begins to tell a story and each person has to continue the story using a word beginning with his letter almost immediately. Some link words are allowed. For example :-

"I went to Africa by boat, crossing difficult estuaries."

The faster the story can be told the better!

Where's the Whistle?

Three or four volunteers are sent out of
sight and earshot of the circle, and the
rest of the audience is asked to form a
perfect circle, that is one which is tight
and unbroken. The leader attaches a whistle
to the back of his belt by a small length
of string. Ideally the whistle is hidden
by a pullover or similar. The members
of the audience are to blow the whistle
whenever the opportunity arises, but they
must do so discreetly in order that the
four volunteers are unable to identify
where the whistle is. The camp fire leader
stands in front of various members of the
audience to make this possible. At the
same time they are to pretend to be passing
round an imaginary whistle behind their
backs and if they are challenged by the
volunteers to be in possession of the
whistle they are to show their empty hands.
The volunteers are brought in one at a
time to try to spot the whistle. They
may soon come to suspect the leader but
for the first couple of challenges he can
always show his empty hands as well.

The Hippopotamus

A highly amusing but difficult technique to master is that of doing something very silly whilst keeping a perfectly straight face. One example of this would be to sing the hippopotamus song "Mud, mud, glorious mud" in a very posh voice. A large Scout might then sing the chorus and a slim Scout (or, better still, a slim dainty Cub Scout Leader) could join in the second chorus. The correspondent who suggested this informed us that the Cubs were invited to sing the last chorus as well, but most of them were laughing so much they could not join in.

The Orchestra is Human

The camp fire circle is divided into segments and each group of people is given the name of a musical instrument such as trumpet, violin, drum, triangle, the base section and so on. A very well known tune is chosen and instead of singing the song the members of the audience hum, sing or "perform" the tune in an appropriate sound to the instrument which they represent. Some practice and final co-ordination may be necessary and the effect can be greatly added to if there is a chorus of male and female members who can harmonise. The job of the camp fire leader is to conduct the proceedings, bringing in different instruments at the appropriate point in the song.

Three Chocolate Eclairs

This song could easily have come into our Bad Taste Section! It is sung to the tune "Two lovely black eyes".

Three chocolate eclairs
Three chocolate eclairs
Three chocolate eclair, air, airs
Sitting on a plate

Action : Gobbling an eclair.

The chorus is repeated with the words "two chocolate eclairs", and the action of gobbling a second eclair. The chorus is again repeated with the words "one chocolate eclair" followed by the action of gobbling a third eclair. The final chorus is "no chocolate eclairs", and the camp fire leader says :

"I don't feel well."

The action is that of being sick!

The song then turns around and the next verse is "one chocolate eclair", the action is being sick again and the verse continues "two chocolate eclairs", the action is being sick again and the verse is "three chocolate eclairs".

BUILDING THE CAMP FIRE

All the previous items in this book have been sent in by a large number of readers of Scouting Magazine and we are greatly indebted to them for this. However, we are particularly grateful to Simon Stockley of the Rydal Hall Service Crew for sending a number of useful items, and particularly some very practical advice on building a successful camp fire.

A camp fire should be built to cater for the following six requirements :-

1) It should light first time.

2) It should burn for one to two hours.

3) It should give sufficient light for stunts.

4) It should be big enough for the anticipated audience.

5) It should provide a mass of hot embers for any late night cooking.

6) Most importantly, it should require no further attention after being lit.

To achieve these points it is important to build the fire with firm foundations. Two large logs should be placed on the ground parallel to each other about three feet apart. Each log should be about four feet long and six to eight inches in diameter. If necessary, the ground should be dug away slightly to prevent them wobbling. The second layer consists of two further logs of similar dimensions placed at right angles to the first layer. The points where the logs meet are notched so that the second layer sits firmly on the first and is unlikely to roll even once some of the surrounding wood has burnt away. The third layer consists of two slightly smaller logs laid at right angles to the second layer.

The space in between these layers is filled with a number of thin, straight sticks approximately one inch in diameter which form the fire grate. The purpose of this layer is to allow air into the base of the fire when it is started. The pyramid is continued upwards with further layers of logs constantly decreasing in size, and still being notched to prevent rolling. The topmost layer will consist of logs about one and a half inches in diameter and one foot long, and will be about four feet from the ground.

Once the timber has been selected and pre-pared the pyramid is dismantled to the level of the fire grate. The centre of the fire is packed with a mixture of kindling, small twigs and small logs to ensure that it catches quickly and stays burning. The function of the kindling and small twigs is to provide an instant flame which will quickly set fire to the larger logs which will burn more slowly. Newspaper may be used but dry bark, leaves and small twigs would be much more effective. The pyramid of the fire is re-built around this filling. Once the fire is built it should be covered with a tarpaulin or similar to ensure that all your hard work is not ruined by a sudden downpour!

If the fire is built along these lines
(although it is not necessary to operate
with a tape measure and slide rule!) the
chances are that a) the fire will light
first time and b) it will burn in a
controlled manner, collapsing inwards,
thereby keeping the audience safe, and
ensuring that it will burn for a good length
of time. If there is any chance that the
fire you have constructed will not burn
for long enough, a supply of logs should
be kept close at hand to avoid a panic
stricken rush for firewood at a crucial
point in the programme.

A CAMP FIRE BLANKET TO MAKE

Obtain an old overcoat from a jumble sale or charity shop, the larger and heavier it is the better. Cut off the sleeves at the shoulders, leaving enough material to sew over the armholes so that they are completely sealed. This gives the beginning of a cape shape to the garment. The front edges can be folded in from the bottom to give a swept back appearance and the lapels can be cut where they join the collar so that the collar can be worn turned up whilst the lapels stay flat. If you are experienced at working with cloth you will be able to make further adaptions to the garment to shape it but this is not really necessary. The basic requirement for a camp fire blanket is a large number of badges, preferably National, County, District and Group badges obtained from other Scouts and events. If you have patience it is advisable to build up a collection of badges before you start to sew them on to the garment so that you can arrange them in some sort of logical pattern. For example, it might be a good idea to sew on the larger triangular pennants round the base of the garment with the points uppermost, followed by the circular badges produced for special events and by particular sites, and then moving up the garment with smaller and smaller badges. You may wish to group the badges by type, i.e. all County badges in one place, District badges in another etc. You may wish to place some particularly significant motif in the centre of the back of the garment. This might be a design bringing out your own name or nickname, or the Scout Badge, or any other symbol you consider appropriate. The garment can be further embellished with bits of fur, coloured ribbons etc. until it has the "personality" that you are looking for.

AND FINALLY

We hope that you have enjoyed reading this book and that you have obtained a number of ideas from it which you will have fun putting into practice. It is important to keep your plans secret from as many people as possible so that the largest number of people can enjoy each stunt. There is not much point in passing this book around the whole Group so that each Section can choose its own stunts for one particular camp fire, only to find that everybody knows the punchline for all the stunts when they are performed!

We hope that this is not the end of the story. We would very much like to produce Camp Fire Stunts 2, 3, 4 and more, but we can only do this if you, the readers, continue to send us your particular favourites. We already have a small supply of stunts which could not be fitted into this edition to start us off and we look forward to a flood of further contributions once this book hits the news stands! Future editions may contain more stunts which are your old favourites and many more which will be new to you, further hints on setting up and running camp fires, examples of different ways of opening and closing proceedings, yells and rounds, further designs for camp fire blankets etc. Who knows, we may even produce a book of camp fire songs if we can sort out the copyright problems!

The address to write to is :   David Saint
                              6 Angel Hill Drive
                              Sutton
                              Surrey SM1 3BX